D1474878

Metro Futures

Metro
Futures

ECONOMIC SOLUTIONS FOR
CITIES AND THEIR SUBURBS

Daniel D. Luria
and Joel Rogers

Foreword by the REVEREND JESSE L. JACKSON, SR.

Edited by Joshua Cohen and Joel Rogers
for *Boston Review*

BEACON PRESS
BOSTON

BEACON PRESS
25 Beacon Street
Boston, Massachusetts 02108-2892
www.beacon.org

Beacon Press books are published under the auspices of the
Unitarian Universalist Association of Congregations.

05 04 03 02 01 00 99   8 7 6 5 4 3 2 1

This book is printed on recycled acid-free paper that contains at least 20
percent postconsumer waste and meets the uncoated paper ANSI/NISO
specifications for permanence as revised in 1992.

Text design by Christopher Kuntze
Composition by Wilsted & Taylor Publishing Services

Library of Congress Cataloging-in-Publication Data

Metro futures : economic solutions for cities and their suburbs /
    [edited by] Daniel D. Luria and Joel Rogers ; foreword by Jesse L.
Jackson, Sr.
        p.   cm. — (New democracy forum)
    Includes bibliographical references.
    ISBN 0-8070-0603-3 (pbk.)
    1. Urban policy—United States.   2. Urban economics.
3. Metropolitan areas—United States.   I. Luria, Dan.   II. Rogers,
Joel, 1952– .   III. Series.
HT123.M417   1999
307.76'0973—DC21   99-28328

Contents

III

Foreword:
Rebuilding Urban America

THE REVEREND JESSE L. JACKSON, SR.

*I*n August 1996, I stood before the nation at the Democratic National Convention, in one of this nation's great cities, Chicago. I spoke of "life in the canyon" in this great city, reminding the delegates of the disinvestment that had gone on in urban America during past decades—of the companies that had moved on seeking lower wages and weaker unions, of the good jobs that had left, of the families destabilized and broken in their wake. Jobs out, drugs in, workers busted.

In every great city I visit, a new ballpark and a new jail. In the canyon, people live with first-class jails and second-class schools. Half of all the public housing built in America: jail cells. The biggest growth industry in urban America: prisons.

Yet the future of America is the future of our cities. Restoring their health and wealth is the key to advancing racial justice, to raising and equalizing wages, to promoting equal opportunity, to saving our environment. It is the key to reversing the mean-spirited, "trickle-down" public policies of the past twenty years, to rebuilding the fabric of our neighborhoods and communities, to strengthening labor and other democratic organizations.

So it is strange that politicians give so little attention to the real problems in our cities. We hear more about the need for prisons than the need to cure the urban poverty and hopelessness that so often lead to crime. We hear more about the need for family discipline than the need to discipline the corporate interests that downsize the workforce, drag down wages, and drive our families apart. We hear all the time why we must sell off or shut down our urban schools, libraries, and parks, while we do nothing to protect the tax base that could support them. We seem to have enough money for new weapons systems, but no money to rebuild crumbling school buildings. We hear about the need to remove protections from open spaces, but not about the costs of sprawl.

And we carry the shame, as a nation, of wasting a generation of America's children, who grow up in poverty in the midst of unprecedented riches.

We are enjoying the longest peacetime period of economic growth in American history, but our people in many parts of the United States—in our urban ghettos and barrios, in Appalachia, in the Mississippi Delta, in the Rio Grande Valley—have not been invited to the party. They are willing to work, but they lack good jobs at decent wages. They lack investment. They lack capital.

We hear so much about emerging markets overseas—in China, and Indonesia, and Burma. Yet we hear so little about the greatest untapped markets of all—our own cities, right here at home. These areas offer millions of prospective consumers and workers with far more resources and higher levels of education than the citizens of so-called emerging markets abroad. It is time to see America's overlooked areas for what they are: rich, untapped markets for U.S. investment, both public and private. If we combine public investment and private incentives, resources for educating the young and for providing literacy training to the less young, then there can be hope for new investment, new jobs, new growth. Hope for rebuilding urban America.

But hope requires vision: without vision, the people perish. That's why this book is so important. Dan Luria and Joel Rogers offer us a new vision. They show us that metropolitan regions are the natural building blocks of a high-wage, low-waste, "high-road" economy of broadly shared prosperity—a prosperity that will strengthen and lift up the floor beneath America's poor and working families rather than continuing to raise the roof for the wealthy.

Metro areas are the right place to start in moving us onto the high road of economic development because that's where the needs are greatest and the possibilities are largest. And that means essentially doing what Luria and Rogers prescribe: campaigning for higher standards on wages and environmental protection, for regional tax equity, for assistance to firms trying to make it onto the high road; for more worker training and protection, more respect for democratic principles in governance of our metro areas, more respect for productive worker and citizen organizations within these areas.

Unfortunately, the new picture Luria and Rogers paint for America—brighter, more hopeful, more prosperous, more equitable, more socially just—is currently a distant dream for the future. Getting from here to there will require a struggle, which means that a number of constituencies long divided from one another will need to come together. But here, too, the authors have set out the beginnings of an answer.

Politically, the essential argument is that we now need to "suburbanize" urban issues. Often in the past I have set forth the proposition that progressives need to "whiten" the face of poverty since most poor people are not black or brown, but white, female, and young. Two-thirds of the poor are children. I have also argued that progressives need to "feminize" the issue of affirmative action; this is not just a black or brown issue because the beneficiaries of affirmative action are often white women.

A similar political logic applies here. For far too long, elites have tended to identify our "urban problems" as "black" problems or "brown" problems: racism has fueled urban distress. But Luria and Rogers show that the dilemmas faced by our cities continue to extend out to largely white suburban neighborhoods and communities.

Instead of thinking of urban areas as just central cities, then, let's talk about *metro* areas and an alliance between central cities and inner-ring and older, working-class suburbs. Putting inner-ring suburbs and older, working-class suburbs together with central cities changes the political equation: this new alliance is a clear majority of the voters. Add in institutional forces with a stake in high-road metro reconstruction—unions, advanced business interests—and groups whose concerns are best addressed through metro revival, like environmentalists, civil rights groups, and advocates for women and the poor. Such a coalition would be a formidable force for good.

By shifting our understanding of urban difficulties, Luria and Rogers help deracialize those issues. At the same time, they show that people of color cannot escape the economic misery they experience in the central city just by moving out into the nearest suburbs. Even if they are welcome, they will not find expanding opportunity there, as these suburban towns are now pressured by the same divestment and sprawl that earlier created problems for the central cities.

We are left, then, with a sensible and hopeful prescription, and a crying need for national and local leadership in implementing it. I do not know exactly where such leadership will come from, what color its face will be, or how soon it will include spokespeople for business as well as labor, and working-class suburban elected officials alongside inner-city mayors.

But I do believe that leadership will emerge, that the rejected stones will become the cornerstones of our urban reconstruction, because—as Dr. King taught us—though the arc of the moral universe is long, it does bend toward justice.

So much of America's future depends on resolving our urban problems and rebuilding our cities. I urge you to read and consider *Metro Futures* because I believe it points us in the right direction. The work of Luria and Rogers offers us a map out of the canyon.

Editors' Preface

JOSHUA COHEN AND JOEL ROGERS

$\mathcal{T}$he aim of the *Boston Review*/Beacon Press New Democracy Forum series is to foster morally serious, politically engaged debate about fundamental issues of the day. Each volume presents proposals about how to improve life in this country, and a more demanding and intellectually honest discussion of those proposals than conventional political arenas permit. The cumulative effect, we hope, will be to expand the range of political options beyond the narrow confines of current national debate.

In an earlier volume in the series, *The New Inequality*, economist Richard Freeman presented an ambitious five-part program for addressing growing income inequality in the United States. One of Freeman's proposals was to "target metropolitan regions as the building blocks of a more egalitarian economy." In this volume, Daniel Luria and Joel Rogers (one of the series' co-editors) explore the promise of such a "metro strategy" for addressing two basic problems: squalid conditions in our urban areas, where millions suffer from material poverty and physical insecurity; and the record levels of economic inequality in the country that have resulted from a generation of wage stagnation. According to Luria and Rogers, metropolitan areas—with their dense concentrations of people, human capital, social networks, and physical infrastructure—are just the right places to focus a national, high-wage, high-skill economic strategy. And that strategy promises to keep the economy improving while reducing economic disparities nationally and vastly improving life in our metro regions.

Luria and Rogers also sketch a political strategy for this metro project, based on coalitions between labor and community, cities and inner-ring suburbs, and parts of metro business and labor. The respondents to the proposals put forth by Luria and Rogers broadly agree on the importance of addressing both inequality and urban decay. But they point to the many large hurdles—of race, class, organizational division, and jurisdictional boundaries—that now stand in the way of such coalition-building efforts. They also question whether a strategy for addressing specifically urban problems should be tied so closely to a more comprehensive project for reversing national economic inequality.

These are important disagreements, worth pursuing. The goal of this Forum is to get them on the table as we all try to figure out the place of more vibrant cities in building a new democracy.

❧ I ❧

Metro Futures

DANIEL D. LURIA AND JOEL ROGERS

Cities and their surrounding inner-ring suburbs—
what we will here call "metro" or "urban" regions[1]—are
the neglected stepchildren of American politics. More
than half the population lives in them, and they suffer
from all sorts of problems, from ghetto crime and unemployment, racial segregation and widening class inequalities, to environmentally degrading and fiscally destabi-
lizing suburban sprawl. Yet in general they are not the
subject of constructive political debate. Instead, discussion of our urban areas usually serves only as an occasion
for expressing despair about economic dysfunction and
social disintegration, and about the resistance of both to
political remedy. The problems of our cities are taken to
be inevitable in origin and now so advanced that they
defy solution.

Such despair is justified, we are told, by an Iron Law
of Urban Decay, which condemns even successful cities
to eventual decline. As incomes rise, workers move to
suburbia; when suburbs mature, they resist paying taxes
to support the metro core; as the tax base declines and
services deteriorate in the city, the middle class flees.

Poverty concentrates among those left behind, and they become "different"—disconnected from labor markets, without role models for advancement, lacking the human or financial capital even for bootstrapping. The best that can be hoped for in the central cities is peace, or at least a segregation of the violence. The best that can be hoped for in suburbia is . . . more suburbia. But further sprawl only erodes the tax base of the inner-ring suburbs, wedging their residents between the spreading deterioration of the urban core and the new roads, sewers, and schools of their increasingly distant suburban "neighbors" further out. Angry inner-ring suburbanites tend to blame their more proximate neighbors in the central cities for their problems—overwhelmingly people poorer and darker than themselves. Meanwhile, the wealthy seek to insulate themselves, taking refuge in luxury urban high-rises, cloistered condo communities, or racially and class exclusionist "favored quarters" of exurban development.

It is an ugly business, all the more so because it does not have to be this way. We could reconstruct our metropolitan regions. Taking full advantage of their dense concentration of people, skill, and infrastructure, we could transform them from sites of hideous squalor, stark inequality, and numbing natural destruction to vibrant centers of high-wage, environmentally sustainable economic activity and civil social life.

The benefits would be massive. Most directly, metro

reconstruction would markedly improve the welfare of urban populations. More broadly, it would substantially address the rising inequality and stagnant wages that have defined American labor markets over the past generation. Finally, since economic realities condition most of the rest of our lives together, such reconstruction would have large political and social benefits. It would be a gain for democracy and social peace in this country —and make more meaningful our now-fragile commitments to shared citizenship—if we actually focused resources and policy attention where most people, including many of the least well off, now live.

Despite these benefits, any serious project of metropolitan reconstruction will mean a fight on several fronts. Winning it will require a wide-ranging alliance of interests: large numbers of people now divided from one another must be persuaded of their common stake in its success. And persuasion depends on having a plausible project capable of uniting these different interests.

The essentials of such a project can be stated. For reasons of space, we present them schematically, without much reference to the particular settings and histories— in cities as diverse as Minneapolis–St. Paul and Portland, Seattle and Cleveland, Chattanooga and Milwaukee—that inspire our confidence in the possibilities of realizing them. While we have included lots of details about what needs to be done and by whom, we also understand that such details are provisional: the best way to proceed will differ from case to case. As projects of this kind unfold, we will all learn more about the relative advantages of alternative strategies. But enough is known now about what works, and what does not, that a new urban agenda can be set forth.[2]

Before getting to that agenda and its politics, however, we need first to make the case that metropolitan reconstruction is worth doing, and that it can in fact be done—that the Iron Law of Urban Decay is an artifact of political choice, not nature.

WHY SAVE CITIES?

How did our cities get into their current mess? There is no simple answer, but a very large piece of the puzzle lies in American public policy. A bias against cities, evident in contemporary public discourse, is a long-standing feature of the American political economy, and this bias plays a central role in our tax code, in major economic development programs, and in government purchasing, housing policies, and other exercises of public power. Its effect is to undermine, and finally to obscure, the natural reasons for saving our cities.

The Anti-Urban Bias

In contrast to that of most developed capitalist nations, American public policy slights urban centers in favor of suburban homes, urban bus and subway riders in favor of suburban automobiles, and urban infrastructure in favor of exurban and rural development projects. Though hard to calculate precisely, the subsidy to non-urban regions is on all counts considerable—tens if not hundreds of billions annually. We have spent trillions building non-metro roads, but nowhere near that on metropolitan ones or mass transit. Federal annual funding for mass transit has never been more than a fifth of the amount spent on highways, and state funding ratios are even more unbalanced. The largest share by far of federal and state economic development support also goes to non-metro programs: more highways, sprawl-supporting infrastructure, exurban tax credits, and low-interest loans for new development outside the cities.

Nor do we require non-metro regions to pay the costs of maintaining the poor and dispossessed—and largely nonwhite—populations left behind by such acts of favoritism. To the contrary. Historically, much of our urban policy has, of course, been deeply racist: consider the exclusionary home mortgage policies of the 1940s and 1950s, the casual destruction of black neighborhoods under the banner of "urban renewal" in the 1960s, and the continued indifference toward discrimination in housing and toward the segregating effects on people of color of new housing standards.

Whether best understood as originating in a genuine concern for promoting growth in non-urban areas, or as

attributable to racism or to a misplaced equation of free-
dom with the automobile, the general effect of many of
our public policies has been to artificially lower the
costs—to individuals and businesses—of living and
working outside or on the outer fringes of our metro regions, while artificially increasing the costs of living and
working within them. The effect is to push investment
out of high-tax, low-service urban areas, and into favored low-tax, high-service suburban quarters, while
concentrating poverty in the central city core and, increasingly, squeezing the working-class suburbs in the
middle.[3]

Why Care?

So public policy substantially reduces the costs of living and investing outside metro areas, and thus encour-
ages people and firms to make those choices. But why
should anyone object?

There are three big reasons.

The first is political morality. Beginning with the basics, democracy is supposed to be "for the people"—*all* of
them. With some 140 million people in our urban areas,
and some 70 million (20 million of them children) in the
declining central cities, anti-urban policies don't qualify
as democratic. Democracy is also supposed to be about
equal opportunity to enjoy a decent life. But we know
that, especially in our central cities, large numbers of

people are exceptionally poor, in receipt of exceptionally bad public services, and subject to exceptional violence. No one disputes the results—in high infant mortality, poor health, stunted development, shattered lives, and heavy grief—or the fact that this state of affairs mocks any pretense that we give all our citizens some equal shot at the American dream. Finally, and most recently, we have claimed that American democracy means racial justice. But even as we have made great progress in removing formal barriers to racial equality, our urban policies have had the effect of drastically limiting the civil rights movement's substantive achievements.

A second set of reasons centers on our health and general quality of life. Suburban sprawl promotes pollution of all kinds, ravages the beauty of our natural environment, ensures the greater stress induced by traffic congestion and longer commute times to work, and, by thinning the shared tax base of our major population centers, undermines our ability to pay for public goods of all kinds, from opportunities for safe recreation to quality public education.

Finally—and less familiarly—anti-urbanism is economically unwise. For starters, the combination of sprawl and central city degradation is wasteful. It wastes land, water, and energy, and squanders existing assets. As new houses, factories, and schools go up in the outer rings of suburbia, perfectly good buildings, with established links to usable infrastructure, get boarded up further in.

Take the excess costs of new construction and the elimination of natural resources, add in the untimely depreciation of old capital stock, and the resultant figure stands at easily $300 billion in annual waste.

Consider also the economic costs of human neglect. In strictly economic terms, abandoning our central cities means forsaking the productive potential of their inhabitants while paying heavily to contain their resentment, as ballooning budgets for new prisons and police make evident. And the "opportunity costs" of all that unrealized productivity are enormous. Forget about the loss of potential Nobel Prize winners. Simply subtract the average lifetime earnings of a person without decent healthcare, education, or job access from the lifetime earnings of someone who enjoys these basic goods. Multiply by 70 million, or even by only 20 million. It's a big number—in the trillions—which translates into a lot of foregone tax revenue for the general population.

Then there is cost linkage. Many suburbanites are prepared to pay the costs and forego the benefits just mentioned as the price of distancing themselves from urban problems. But that distance is an illusion. Within metro regions, the economic fortunes of central cities and those of their suburbs, especially their inner-ring suburbs, are increasingly entwined. By the late 1980s, across a very wide range of metro regions, every $1,000 gained or lost in per capita city income was associated with a corresponding $690 gain or loss in per capita suburban income.[4] Rotting central cities mean a poorer suburban future.

The really big economic cost of urban decay, however, derives from the role that metro regions play in determining the pattern of national economic activity. Put baldly, revived urban regions are key to reversing the present stagnation in American living standards. This is a large claim: defending it will require that we step back briefly from cities and consider the state of the national economy.

PAVING THE HIGH ROAD

Despite all the talk about how American wages are now set in Beijing, adverse trends in American income (including income distribution) today result less from the downward pressures of international competition than from domestic policy choices.[5] Specifically, we have made "low-road" strategies of response to new competitive pressures too easy and "high-road" strategies too hard. Low-road firms compete by keeping prices down, which means keeping costs down—beginning, typically, with wages. Applied across the economy, low-road strategies lead to sweated workers, economic insecurity, rising inequality, poisonous labor relations, and degraded natural environments. High-road firms focus on "value competition," with higher wages supported by customer willingness to pay for higher quality, better design, and superior service, and they require continual innovation in quality; thus they depend on more skilled and more cooperative workers. In general, high-road strategies are associated with higher productivity, higher pay and better labor relations, reduced environmental damage, and greater corporate commitment to the health and stability of surrounding human communities—all needed to attract and keep skilled workers and managers.

Firms can make money on either path, but social gains are vastly greater on the high road. The principal failure of the past two decades—and it is political as much as economic—is that we have not done what we must to move the economy toward it. Embarking on the high road is associated with various transition costs, and staying on it requires a variety of social supports. These supports include effective educational and training institutions; better functioning labor markets, with fuller information about requirements for job access and advancement; advanced infrastructure of all kinds; modernization services to diffuse the best manufacturing practices; and, throughout, barriers to low-road defection (high and rising wage, safety, or environmental performance floors, for example). Because such supports typically lie beyond the capacity of individual firms, they need to be provided socially. We have not provided them, and the results are clear in the sorry labor-market and productivity data of the last couple of decades—

data which show stagnating or falling wages, rising inequality, and anemic productivity growth.

Cities and the High Road

This brings us back to the cities and to the importance of saving them. Whatever their present difficulties, metropolitan economies are the natural base for a high-road economy. In fact, those high-road production and service enterprises that do exist in the United States are already disproportionately concentrated in metropolitan regions. This concentration is no accident. A high-road strategy must almost surely be a metro strategy because the high road generally requires the sheer density of people and firms found only in cities.

The affinity between metro density and "highroading" is expressed in three ways. First, density facilitates worker organization by providing the proximity and sheer numbers needed to support the infrastructure necessary for member servicing and for new organizing efforts. Worker organization, in turn, directly helps to close off the low road by obstructing the impulse to reduce wages. And worker organization helps pave the high road, too. Without the knowledge and cooperation of workers, companies and corporations will find highroading all but impossible—and both are easier to secure if workers are organized and confident that they too will benefit from increased quality and productivity.

Density also helps firms more directly. Economists, geographers, and economic development analysts use the concept of "agglomeration" to describe the benefits in skills, productivity, and consumer access that result when activities are concentrated in particular places. Firms in such areas don't just happen to be near each other and share a regional labor market: they do business with each other in a way that connects them as if, in some ways, they were complementary parts of a single enterprise. At the extreme, some of their capacity may even be thought of as shared. Precisely because they want to keep their machinery busy, each firm has strong incentives to make overflow work available to "competitors," since by doing so they may earn the *quid pro quo* of having the favor returned.

Agglomerations are in turn associated with "increasing returns" on any given investment. When a single firm in one of these agglomerations improves its cost and quality performance, it creates a competitive advantage for all the customers and suppliers in its cluster. Simply put, firms learn more and faster from each other.[6]

Finally, density helps relieve the costs of providing the public goods upon which advanced production depends: education and training; formal supports for cross-learning and upgrading among firms; integrated regional labor market services and worker credentialing systems; and modern forms of transport, energy and

{ 14 }

water supplies, and communications. It is much cheaper and easier to supply such goods in the context of the concentration of human and material resources that density provides.

Put all this together, and it's easy to see why metro regions historically offered, and still hold the promise of extending, a virtuous cycle of earnings-led productivity growth. Agglomeration, especially when it includes a sectoral mix that favors high-skill labor, is a clear predictor of higher employee earnings. These higher earnings justify and call forth a higher level of capital investment per employee. High labor quality and high capital intensity beget higher productivity, which supports continued premium labor compensation. This in turn attracts skilled employees in both manufacturing and services, and the whole virtuous cycle repeats. Nor, we stress, is this cycle a thing of the past. It persists today. As *Business Week* recently reported, "Cities still seem best able to provide business with access to skilled workers, specialized high-value services, and the kind of innovation and learning growth that is facilitated by close contact between diverse individuals."[7]

The Case of Manufacturing

The story of the past and present importance of metro regions economically, and the destructive effects of sprawl-promoting policies, can be told for many sectors

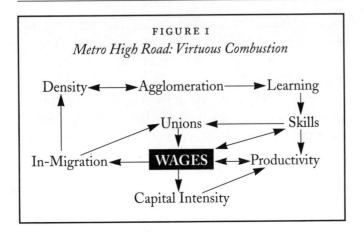

FIGURE I
Metro High Road: Virtuous Combustion

of the economy. We tell it here for manufacturing, an important driver of general wage patterns and the demand for advanced services, and a sector of particular importance to the populations of people of color most clearly brutalized by the present urban decline.[8]

Let's begin by operationalizing the definition of "high-road" and "low-road" for firms within this sector. We concentrate on those firms employing fewer than five hundred workers which make up better than 98 percent of all factories in the United States and employ nearly six in ten manufacturing workers. Data gathered by the Performance Benchmarking Service (PBS) show that roughly one-third of such firms have productivity, measured as value-added per employee, of less than $50,000, while another third have productivity above

$90,000. Of the latter group, about half, or 15 percent of the total, have productivity exceeding $100,000. And about two-thirds of that 15 percent (hence 10 percent of the total) have productivity above $110,000 (which is the average for plants with *more* than five hundred employees).

For the purposes of this analysis, we are calling "low-road" all shops in the bottom half of this distribution, or those with value-added per employee of $70,000 or less; "high-road" shops are those in the top 15 percent, with value-added per employee exceeding $100,000. Such high-road firms, again, are good not only for workers but for owners too. The PBS data show that plants that achieve $100,000 in value-added per employee pay yearly wages and benefits of about $45,000 (think $16–$18/ hour wages, plus good benefits)—nearly double those of plants achieving at the $50,000 productivity level—and are nearly 50 percent more profitable.

Still, today the same PBS data show that high-road shops are adding sales and hence employment at slower rates than low- and mid-road shops. The main culprit is what economists call capacity utilization. High-road shops are, on average, twice as capital intensive as low-roaders. When orders are strong, higher capital costs per unit of output and higher wages per hour are both easily outweighed by superior labor productivity. But when orders decline, high fixed costs and high wages quickly translate into a squeeze on profits.

And why are orders less certain today? Simply put, high-road shops are not doing exclusively high-road work: in order to keep their expensive machinery busy, they also take on orders that lower-road competitors can adequately perform. Thus when lower-roaders undercut their bids on these easier-to-make products, the high-roaders' capacity utilization plummets, and with it their profitability. As a matter of public policy, through drops in the minimum wage, deregulation, attacks on unions, etc., we have helped to pave the low road in manufacturing. And low-roaders find a market in the purchasing departments of major corporations. Just as Taylorism enjoyed a half-century of success "unbundling" the tasks that, when bundled, created a set of skilled trades, so today the purchasing function of major corporations works tirelessly to maximize that portion of their production processes that can be treated as a commodity and hence priced through competitive bidding. Thus lower-road shops enjoy a growing opportunity to bid away the easier-to-make portion of the high-roaders' order books.

If high-road firms are thus challenged, those just beneath them are also tempted to choose the low road. PBS data show that plants that achieve $80,000 in value added per employee provide wage and benefit compensation of nearly $40,000, but are on average barely more profitable than low-roaders achieving only $50,000 productivity levels. In other words, the high road must be truly high to provide both good jobs to employees and

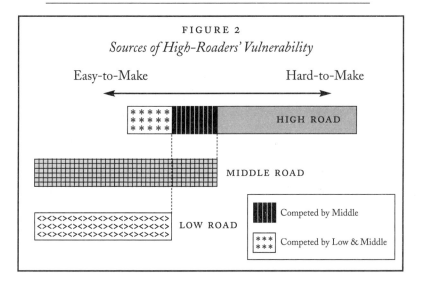

FIGURE 2

Sources of High-Roaders' Vulnerability

Easy-to-Make   Hard-to-Make

HIGH ROAD

MIDDLE ROAD

LOW ROAD

■ Competed by Middle

✳✳✳ Competed by Low & Middle

competitive rewards to the owners of capital. But with few incentives to embark on the high road, and no bar to pursuing the easier low one, few firms make the transition to the higher level. More commonly, they set about the process of reducing worker wages and benefits, cutting back on investment in new plants and equipment, reducing training, and otherwise sinking to low-road production methods and industrial relations.

What does all this have to do with cities, and the competition between metropolitan and exurban locations? Plenty. For the reasons given above, high-road manufacturing is disproportionately urban. To trash our urban areas, then, is to undermine our high-road manufacturing base.

To see the metro bias of the high road, consider the distribution of high- and low-road production by sector and location. High-road manufacturing firms cluster heavily in the production of capital goods—machinery, equipment, tools, dies, and patterns. Along with end-use products, these account for better than 85 percent of what they make. Low-roaders, by contrast, concentrate on easier-to-make intermediate goods of various kinds; along with a heftier share of end-use products, such goods account for close to 95 percent of what they make.

Now consider sectors by location. Capital goods companies are more than four times as likely as the average manufacturing firm to be metro. For truly high-end sectors, the numbers are even more striking. Better than 90 percent of all tool-and-die shops, for example, are in metro areas. By contrast, intermediate goods producers are, as a group, significantly more likely to be rural, and reduced transportation costs (which in the United States are mainly a result of trucking deregulation) and improved telecommunications have made this more and more the case since the mid-1970s.

Also consider the associated metro manufacturing wage effect. A 1989 analysis found that in 1986 workers in the thirty-eight "densest" manufacturing MSAs (areas somewhat wider than the "urban" or "metro" areas that are our focus here) enjoyed payroll per employee that averaged 19 percent higher than in the rest of the economy, and that this pay premium was present, on average, in firms of all sizes. By 1997, this premium had eroded but still stood at a respectable 13 percent; moreover, virtually all of the erosion reflected the growth in low-road manufacturing jobs in outer-ring suburbs rather than an erosion in wages in urban capital-goods shops.[9]

But if metro manufacturing is thus disproportionately high-road manufacturing, what are we doing to it? Essentially, we are destroying it.

How the anti-urban bias of public policy plays in the manufacturing area is recorded in figure 3. From peak to peak in the business cycle from 1978 to 1988, just sixteen central cities shed a mind-boggling 1.3 million jobs, or about a third of their manufacturing base and close to seven in ten of all manufacturing jobs lost nationally. Over roughly the same period, inner-ring suburbs also suffered heavy manufacturing losses. Given the much higher rates of unionization in urban areas, this urban deindustrialization was also associated with massive deunionization of the manufacturing sector nationally.

There has been some qualified good news since. While the period after 1988 has continued to see declines in manufacturing employment, the sixteen hard-hit cities have not on average suffered declines much steeper than those experienced by the rest of the nation. Over the period from 1988 to 1997, they lost another 205,000 jobs, or 7.4 percent of their base, while other areas gained 456,000 jobs, or 2.9 percent. Urban manufacturing is still not holding its own, but the rate of decline has been cut by about 80 percent. And even today, those sixteen areas that suffered intense deindustrialization in the 1980s are home to better than 50 percent of all of those tool-

FIGURE 3
Metro Deindustrialization

Metro Manufacturing Employment (millions)

	1978	*1988*	*% Change*	*Share of Total Loss*
16 Cities	4.1	2.8	-32.4%	69%
Everywhere Else	16.2	15.6	-3.8	31
Total	20.3	18.4	-9.5	100

Union and Non-Union Manufacturing (millions)

	1980	*1990*	*% Change*
Union	6.7	4.2	-37.6%
Non-Union	13.6	14.9	+9.7

Inner-Ring Manufacturing (1980–90)

	Detroit	*Milwaukee*
Inner City	-39.1%	-32.5%
Inner Suburbs	-31.1	-18.1
Outer Suburbs	-11.3	6.5

and-die shops associated with high-roading, along with countless other advanced production firms. However much we're doing our best to destroy it, high-road metro manufacturing is far from gone. In this sector, as in others, the metro advantage—in wages, productivity, and even profits—is still there. It's just diminishing in relative weight as we continue to kill our cities.

METRO RECONSTRUCTION

But are metro regions really viable? What would it take to repeal the Iron Law, end the anti-urban bias of public policy, capture the natural advantages of density, and turn our policies more deliberately to building the infrastructure for high-road competition? Besides political will (to which we return later), we need a new array of policies for federal and state governments, and, coordinated with them, a new set of priorities for economic regions.

At the federal and state levels of government, the essential tasks are to keep states and communities from pursuing a competitive race to the bottom, to raise minimum standards on corporate performance, and to get out of the way of the organizing needed to realize gains from cooperation. None of this need imply any new public expenditures.

Federal and state governments could simply do the following.

1. Remove subsidies to low-roading firms. Government bodies should announce that they will not award contracts or development grants to firms paying wages below some minimum level (say, sub-poverty wages), or polluting the environment above a certain level, or having a record of illegal resistance to worker organization. They should then move to mandate such standards generally and to gradually raise them. For example, phasing in a significantly increased minimum wage—say, to $10 an hour within five years, as many "living wage" campaigns are demanding—would do wonders for shutting down the low-road option and requiring firms to compete by improving quality. (Of course, there is no point in urging firms on to a high road only to push them off a cliff. So this first element must be understood and treated as part of the larger project.)

2. Discourage "bidding wars" between and within states. State and local governments routinely spend billions simply to lure businesses from one region to another, with no net gain for the national economy. One way to discourage this practice would be to tax any government bids at the next highest level of government (the federal government taxing the states, the states their local governments), or to condition aid from those higher government entities on a lower one's participation in "non-aggression pacts" with peers. Of course, one region's "subsidy" is another's "investment for the future." So we need criteria to distinguish genuine investment that might also be expected to attract businesses—for example, spending for better educational systems—from direct payoffs and abatements.

3. Target development supports to regions on a per capita basis. As a general rule of public policy, we should spend the money where the people are, thus encouraging local governments to increase density rather than avoid it. And let the natural agglomerations of people and firms be rewarded by letting them recapture their individual tax dollars for collective self-improvement. Here, too, there are important issues of design—not having incentives to agglomeration so intense as to encourage insupportable population growth within regions, for example. But progress toward *per capita* equalization is reasonable on economic and social, as well as democratic grounds.

4. Encourage the growth of economic development authorities on a functional, regional basis. While more than half the population lives in metro regions, only 6 percent is subject to any significant metro governance. Moreover, the sheer number of sovereign sub-jurisdictions in these regions commonly poses formidable barriers to planning. The Chicago metropolitan region, for example, includes 265 separate municipalities, 1,200 separate tax districts, and parts of 6 different mega-counties. State and federal governments could condition aid on the development of regional administrative structures lower down. In very few cases is there actual dispute about the boundaries of the regional economy; the problem has been an absence of national or state leadership in fostering regional frameworks for economic development and planning.

5. Directly encourage high-roading. In all aspects of economic development spending—infrastructure support, pollution prevention and abatement programs, and the like—government should reward regions or states that move toward high-road production. Comparative progress toward the high road can and should be measured, with special federal monies contingent on achieving progress. Independent of what the states do, the federal government should itself be much more attentive to targeting its resources to encourage high-roading. It should target aid to integrated regions, clusters within them, and firms within those clusters.

Together, these five elements would work to remove the anti-urban and low-road bias from contemporary state and federal policy; they would encourage eighteenth- and nineteenth-century jurisdictions to consider the realities of early twenty-first-century regional economic interdependence; and they would encourage both firms and regions to exploit the advantages of density.

And, again, many of these steps would save public monies—by removing economically inefficient or destructive public subsidies, or encouraging greater effi-

ciency in transportation and infrastructure spending—
while most others could be done by simply redirecting
existing expenditures rather than requiring new ones.
Take, as just one example, the case of metro manufacturing considered earlier. The lead federal agency for
"manufacturing extension"—the upgrading of quality
and productivity in those fewer-than-five-hundred-
employee manufacturing firms considered—spends
$200 million annually and touches ten thousand plants.
In general, however, the services provided through its
affiliate centers (advice on quality certification, plant
layout, and the adoption of "lean" manufacturing tech-
niques) are most useful to low- and mid-road shops trying to hold down their quotes for commodity orders, not
to "challenged" high-roaders trying to get to over the
productivity hump needed for real profit gains. There is
nothing natural or necessary in this. We know, with
some precision, those things that make high-road manufacturing different.[10] It would certainly be possible to as-
semble a package of services and supports to help get
firms to that different point, and to target these supports
to the metro areas where our potential high-road base is
most evident. Again, as a matter of public policy, we have
simply chosen not to do this.

And when one considers the gains to be had from doing so, or adopting any of these other remedial steps, that
is really unwise.

Rethinking Regional Rules

Higher levels of government, however, can only do so much to foster metro reconstruction. To be sure, moving the national economy onto a high road would be of manifest national benefit. But because a high-road policy must be a metro policy, regions themselves must play a large role in designing and implementing it. What should metro regions do?

The short answer is that they need to break squarely with the conventional economic development strategy (hereafter, CEDS) still pursued by most cities and counties—the strategy that lies behind the Iron Law of Decay—in favor of a high-road project that takes full advantage of metro density. Let's distinguish CEDS and our alternative on five dimensions.

1. What kind of jobs? CEDS adapts to urban decline by promoting job growth without concern for the kind of jobs generated. But low-wage jobs drag down wages elsewhere, encourage further low-roading, eat away at the margin of struggling high-road firms, and draw on the tax base (low-wage employers still need basic infrastructure, and the employees who occupy low-wage jobs still need basic services) without proportionately contributing to it. Tax-base erosion, in turn, leads to cutbacks in public goods and suburban flight—the Iron Law again. Nevertheless, this strategy is perversely self-enforcing: as the city gets more squalid, desperation fuels the view that jobs, any jobs at all, are what is needed, and that the only alternative to low-wage employment is no employment at all.

A natural alternative is to direct dollars only to jobs of a certain kind, while building supports for them. Localities should make it easier for "good" employers to stay and expand by providing a variety of services and opportunities for their improvement and competitiveness, while making it harder for "bad" employers to do so by insisting on certain standards on wages, pollution prevention, and so on. The architects of such a policy could start by setting conditions on the receipt of government contracts and economic development supports, and then —supported by our new state and federal framework discouraging a "race to the bottom" between regions— move on to mandates on private activity.

2. Attraction or retention? CEDS focuses on attracting businesses rather than retaining and renewing the existing base of firms. It squanders one of the greatest assets of density, which is the natural grouping of similar firms—drawn together by cross-learning, joint production, and the other mutual supports that proximity provides—in distinct industries or industry clusters. Mature metropolitan economies thrive when their core businesses upgrade, link to one another, or attract or spin off related enterprises that benefit from spatial proximity to existing industry leaders. But, as emphasized earlier, upgrading, networking, and incubating indigenous firms requires an infrastructure of support (technical assistance, training, and the efficient supply of modern public goods).

Our alternative development strategy would focus on retention, renewal, upgrading, linkage, and incubation of existing firms, with local authorities investing in the infrastructure needed to realize gains from agglomeration. Through "early warning/early intervention" networks, these local authorities would recruit firms and workers to monitor the signs of distress in challenged firms, and to develop the technical and financial intervention wherewithal to save jobs worth saving. At the same time, they would actively promote cross-firm learning and sectoral growth by encouraging firms to join together in marketing their products and training workers. Drawing on the accumulated pension and other savings in the region, they would develop regional investment funds to support such intervention, increase community ownership of firms doing business there, and support promising spin-offs and incubation centers.

3. Generic or targeted benefits? CEDS relies on generic tax abatements and other fiscal giveaways, rather than targeted breaks and regulation. Again, the best evidence shows that such enterprise zone–type development models simply do not work, and that they eventually erode the city's fiscal base. The jobs generated are seldom high-paying or associated with significant capital investment; the firms take the benefits and move on.

In contrast, much evidence suggests that by a gradual tightening of regulatory controls on production standards—whether minimum labor costs or emissions standards—businesses can be encouraged to innovate in ways that improve both productivity and the quality of community life. Doing this, however, requires a willingness to impose significant costs on current businesses, while insulating them from competition from noncomplying competitors.

Our alternative would set performance conditions on the receipt of public funds—tying subsidies to the achievement of specific ends—and "claw back" those funds from firms that do not meet the conditions. The more extensive the support from government and allied private institutions, of course, the more extensive the demands that could reasonably be made on the firms receiving it would be.

4. What role for markets? The proponents of CEDS see greater public control and accountability as bad for the economy, and they worry when unions and community organizations put pressure on economic policy. Starting from the largely correct perception that government and the general public are ill-prepared to instruct business on how best to achieve particular standards or ends, they arrive at the incorrect conclusion that they are therefore incapable even of specifying them.

Yet modern economies operate best when they can rely on a fair degree of public support for business goals

—support best achieved when the public has significant say in setting those goals. Design and construction of an effective training and credentialing system, for example, requires local knowledge of a variety of distinct service and production settings. The state is commonly at a loss in confronting such issues, as are individual firms. Unions and employer associations, with detailed knowledge across particular sites and the ability to compel performance within them, are critical to success.

Our alternative would continue to let markets do what they do best—allocate scarce resources efficiently and punish the non competitive—but would be unabashed in allowing public authority and popular organizations to have a say in what the goals of economic activity should be. Breaking with both "live free or die" and "private markets versus public hierarchies" models of regulation, it would explicitly assign a role in economic administration to representative nongovernmental institutions (again, unions, employer organizations, community organizations) with local knowledge or other capacity not found in government itself. In our examples above, it might give substantial control over resources for skill training to sectoral training consortia, or control of the early warning network to responsible area unions.

5. Public goods? CEDS neglects the role that public goods of many kinds—from the traditional "economic" ones of transportation, technical assistance, and education and training to the "social" ones of recreation, safety, and clean environments—play in a local economy. In terms of understanding this issue, local economic development efforts lag behind most advanced businesses, which rely on the economic goods for production and the social goods to attract and retain a skilled workforce and managerial personnel. Since no individual firm is able to provide these economic and social goods on its own, the decision about whether or not to maintain and/or develop the infrastructure that supports them is among the most crucial that local economic development authorities can make. But the ability of such authorities to provide this kind of infrastructure depends directly on the population of high-roading firms and associations with a stake in it: the failure to provide decent infrastructure will drive that population down to the point that local and regional authorities will be able to attract *only* low-road firms.

Instead of neglecting high-road infrastructure, our alternative would build it. Sometimes this would mean serious investment—in effective transit systems connecting job seekers to workplaces throughout the region, for instance, or the provision of training. More often, it would simply mean fostering cooperation among existing interests or convening players who know what the problems are and have the collective resources to solve many of them but heretofore have had no incentive or support from public authorities to join together to address them. In our model, government would say, in effect, "Here's a problem that we all know exists. You design a feasible solution accountable to the following values and show us how to pay for it, and we will pass a law making sure nobody defects from the necessary deal."

Consider the effects of systematically pursuing our program. Sprawl would be reduced, planning capacity would rise, wages would increase and inequalities decrease, neighborhoods would become less segregated and safer, and public goods would be more abundant: democracy would more evidently show its contribution to the economy. And the strategy would be self-reinforcing. As subsidies to sprawl decrease, the attractions of metropolitan locations rise. As investment returns to metro cores, productivity within them increases, making higher wages more affordable. As organization of the real cluster basis of the economy proceeds, standards for job entry and advancement can be formalized and publicized, which helps to equalize wages. Better wages secure the tax base; this helps pay for the expensive public goods that both further reduce inequality and attract high-roading firms. With more abundant public goods and better job access, central-city residents look less "different" and therefore more desirable as employees. Finally, with greater regional power over something employers really want—skilled labor, infrastructure, technical assistance, credit—the ability of regions to enact standards and discipline "free-riders" and defectors from common regional norms (on fair housing and hiring, land use, tax equity and base-sharing, for example) rises.

WHO CAN DO IT?

But who could put all this together? And is there any reason to think they might make the effort?

Across the country, you can already find different pieces of the project we have recommended. A few regions do have metropolitan government, sensible planning policies, tax-base sharing between rich and poor neighborhoods within the same region, and/or regional standards on zoning (including, critically, fair-housing policies that put poor and disadvantaged populations next to opportunity). Many cities and counties, and some states, have passed "living wage" or "anti–subsidy abuse" legislation that places enforceable conditions on the receipt of public development monies. More are now engaged in serious discussions to curb destructive sprawl. Many local planning and development departments have begun to target their resources toward the improvement of existing clusters of firms. Dozens of communities are trying to bring more order and purpose to dysfunctional education and training programs, by connecting them more closely to organized employer and union input about the training really needed for entry positions and about the standards and supports needed to permit workers to advance out of dead-end jobs. And there are countless "visioning" exercises—which work more or less effectively to unite diverse communities within regions—to establish benchmarks on regional performance and begin discussion of the requisite infrastructure.

But these efforts remain exceptions and importantly qualified in their effects. Faced with continued low-roading competition, they are hard to sustain. None are comprehensive in terms of putting the governance, planning, finance, standards, supports, and popular organization pieces together. None enjoy the appropriate range of supports needed from the state and federal governments. Few, therefore, have reached critical mass, tipping the dynamics of their regions.

Still, the fact that so many initiatives are already in motion, from diverse quarters—some led by local government officials themselves, others by business, labor, or community groups, or particular issue advocates—suggests a wide-ranging potential alliance out there, waiting to be organized. To appreciate its potential, consider the different urban political forces that have been at each others' throats for so many years but are now coming to recognize the limits of mutual antagonism.

The old political/economic strategies, which still dominate the current scene, pit labor against community, the employed against environmentalists, and central cities against inner-ring suburbs, while obscuring relevant divisions within the business community and letting the rich exurbs off too cheaply. But many of the mutual antagonists in this old politics are beginning to see the advantage of cooperation and to take an interest in alliance. White-dominated labor unions increasingly recognize that their declining city membership no longer suffices to protect their workers against low-wage privatization and the destruction of regional labor market standards, let alone to assure the public investments needed to support high-wage production and services. Organized labor needs the voting support of (heavily disorganized) central-city African-American, Latino, and Asian populations: to get that support, it will need to open itself fully to them. These populations, in turn, know better than to count on an increased welfare effort or an expanded public sector. They need private-sector investment and jobs in their communities, and access to jobs elsewhere, and they need those jobs to pay a living wage. Increasingly, they recognize that these things are more likely to be achieved if they are allied with unions—just as unions have found that they can only defend the interests of their members by getting involved in decisions about technology, product strategy, investment, and work organization, and environmentalists have come to recognize that moving from pollution abatement to source reduction requires a presence inside the corporate world.

Inner-ring suburbanites, whose kids are also joining gangs and who are in many cases losing employment at faster rates than the central cities, are learning that the same low-wage sprawl that has almost destroyed the urban center is now destroying them. And both central-city and inner-ring communities recognize their common interest in getting the rich outer suburbs to carry their share of regional burdens. Finally, metro business itself, at least that part of it that cannot easily flee, is interested in kicking out the CEDS supports from beneath the low-roaders now competing for their orders.

Put these forces together in any metro region—and the program outlined here has a real chance of benefiting all of these constituencies—and you have a powerful political coalition. While obstacles remain, material self-interest strongly supports this grand coalition. And recent experience in mobilizing directly on that self-interest—in Milwaukee, the Twin Cities, and Los Angeles, among many other places—suggests the possibilities of a genuinely cross-class and multiracial movement. What is most urgently needed is leadership—some enterprising politicians, labor leaders, savvy community organizers, or sensible metro businesspeople to get in front of a parade that's waiting to form.

If people get organized, elected officials can be made to follow. Winning the relevant state and federal policy supports demands an alliance of those who represent city and inner-ring suburban communities—still, in combination, a clear majority in Congress and most state legislatures—to press the general interest against recalcitrant rich suburbanites and low-road firms. If the general interest doesn't move these delegations, the fact that their respective constituencies are getting unfairly and jointly savaged should. Someone should invite our currently divided metro officials into a room together, show them a few numbers, and point to the large mixed crowd of voters preparing to march outside.

Heal Thyself as Well

BRUCE KATZ

*D*aniel Luria and Joel Rogers expand upon the growing literature that recognizes the costs of metropolitan growth patterns and the potential for new, majoritarian coalitions to design more livable and sustainable cities and suburbs. They recognize that the rapid decentralization underway in the United States is not inevitable but is rather the result of a complex mix of factors, including government policies. In their unique contribution, they link the issues driving a reexamination of metropolitan growth (increasing intra-metropolitan fiscal disparities, the rise of concentrated poverty in distressed communities, the decline of inner suburbs, the loss of open space) to the effect of market forces and government policies on incomes and wages.

The scope of the reforms and the challenges to coalition building that the authors have outlined are formidable. Yet, encouragingly, efforts are underway to curb sprawling development patterns, promote reinvestment in older established communities, and provide working families greater access to educational and economic opportunity.

Clearly, there are many challenges to achieving the

vision contained in this article. Some observers focus on the difficulty of building coalitions that cross jurisdictional, disciplinary, class, racial, and partisan lines. Other critics point to those constituencies (such as real estate and transportation interests) who have benefited substantially from current growth patterns and can be expected to fight any shift in government policies with great vigor.

Ironically, the central cities themselves—which stand to benefit substantially from a shift towards metropolitan policies—may pose some of the greatest challenges to achieving a new metropolitan agenda. Why is this so? First, urban leaders are not fully engaged in wider metropolitan and state efforts to change core policies that affect transportation, land use, and taxation. These leaders—buoyed by downturns in crime and poverty rates, and by surges in employment and home ownership rates—are mostly focused inward on sustaining and accelerating the "comeback" of their cities without regard for the larger metropolitan context.

The cities, in short, do not feel the sense of crisis that is needed to lift political and policy action to the metropolitan level. It is true that cities are better off relative to where they were five, ten, or fifteen years ago. Yet they are losing ground to their suburbs (and, increasingly, to their outer suburbs in particular) in the competition for jobs and middle-class households, and the tax revenues that they represent.

There are, of course, exceptions. Mayor Wellington Webb has helped to form a metropolitan mayors' caucus in Denver; Chicago Mayor Richard Daley has done the same for his city. Chicago business leaders are spearheading a Metropolis Project that touches on disparate issues: education, transportation, land use, and economic competitiveness. And philanthropic foundations like MacArthur, Gund, Heinz, Irvine, and Turner are supporting metropolitan efforts in their respective communities. Yet, for the most part, urban leaders are focused on traditional revitalization agendas and have failed to recognize the power of—or to join—such burgeoning metropolitan coalitions.

Second, the utter dysfunction of many urban systems and bureaucracies (those concerned with schools, labor relations, land assembly, and infrastructure repair, for example) presents a strong bar to realizing the reinvestment side of the metropolitan agenda—a bar that increased tax revenue alone will not cure. Curbing sprawl will not necessarily mean that urban businesses will decide to stay in the city or that suburban businesses may actually relocate there. Even without current government subsidies, the suburbs are easier, cheaper, more predictable places to do business. In most places, doing business with or within the city is still a headache—which costs time, money, and precious resources.

The same goes for families, particularly for families with children. Almost any parent who has a range of housing choices is going to live where schools are high-performing and well financed. Urban public schools simply cannot compete on these grounds—partly because of the high concentration of poor students, partly because of decades of centralization, regimentation, and bureaucratic waste.

The metropolitan agenda described by Luria and Rogers, therefore, needs to be complemented and supplemented by an urban reform agenda of equal magnitude and emphasis. Urban leaders need to recognize, first and foremost, the changing role of their cities within larger regional economies and the changing role that regions play on cross-border issues like transportation, environmental quality, and workforce and economic development.

A recognition of the bigger picture should naturally be followed by local revitalization strategies that go far beyond the downtown efforts currently in vogue. City leaders need to fix the basics—schools, public safety and public service agencies, tax structures—so that they can retain and attract business investment and middle-class residents. They need to forge competitive strategies that build on fixed institutions (such as universities and existing business clusters), restore neighborhood markets, and generate new employment opportunities in growing, high-wage sectors of the economy. They need to link neighborhoods and neighborhood residents to the growth sectors within their regional economies and help provide the supports (transportation, child care, job training) that make these connections possible.

In pursuing these reforms, cities need to take the high road to governing in the same way that Luria and Rogers recommend they take the high road to job creation. Government monopolies—in schools, public housing, employment services, and the like—have proven to be nonresponsive to city residents, particularly to those residents with the fewest resources and the least political clout. Cities need to rethink how they deliver their services. I would suggest that these services could be better delivered in part through an expanded network of community and church institutions and private-sector firms, in part through a different set of tools and rules.

In short, metropolitan solutions alone will not save cities. Cities—through go-it-alone politics, narrow revitalization strategies, and fragmented and ossified bureaucracies—have made their own contributions to the Iron Law of Urban Decay. That law will not be broken unless and until cities themselves change.

Political Barriers

J. PHILLIP THOMPSON

$\mathcal{D}$an Luria and Joel Rogers present a compelling vision of how we can revitalize our national economy by paying attention to our existing growth centers (mainly in cities), raising wage levels through union organizing, and popularizing debate on economic and fiscal policies. Their article "Metro Futures" amply demonstrates the economic irrationality of many government development policies. However, it suggests that a "parade" is just "waiting to form" for the New Urban Agenda, and that all that is needed are "enterprising politicians, labor leaders, savvy community organizers, or sensible metro businesspeople to get in front." This view underestimates the political barriers to implementing a metropolitan vision. Moreover, it is unclear to me how the New Urban Agenda will address issues of racial difference and persistent poverty.

Luria and Rogers emphasize that anti-urban policies violate the "democratic" principle that policy should be "for the people" because the majority of Americans live in urban areas. However, our political system includes anti-majoritarian institutions. The U.S. Senate is a prime example. Each state elects two senators, regardless of the size of its population. Senators from small and sparsely populated rural states wield disproportionate influence in the Senate, generally against urban interests. Similarly, governors are elected by the voters of states that are irrational as economic units, whose suburban and rural populations often combine forces to the political detriment of cities. While government development policies may not be economically rational or politically democratic, they are consistent with the way we structure politics. These long-standing political structures, and many of the politicians that inhabit them, are a forceful voice against change. It is therefore hard to imagine a New Urban Agenda without fundamental political reform.

The vast majority of the nation's elected officials are state and local legislators. They number in the hundreds of thousands. A majority of them represent urban districts, and a sizable fraction of those are in central cities. Given their sheer numbers, urban legislators would appear to be natural advocates for the Urban Agenda. So if the distribution of state economic benefits is as prejudicial as Luria and Rogers maintain, why aren't urban legislators crying out across the country?

I offer several explanations. First, state legislators tend to be quite parochial, in part because they are individually elected from geographically small districts. They have small budgets and can seldom afford to hire policy experts, nor do they have the capacity to monitor the mammoth bureaucracies and complex regulations that shape policy. Given majority-vote rules and the veto power of governors over state legislatures, legislators from cities can have an impact only when they band together. Often they do not.

These factors converge to engender a cumulative self-reinforcing negative political culture, one that I call "retrograde representation." Lacking policy staff or policy resources, it is hard for legislators to know what to advocate. Without a policy vision, there is little basis for forming stable political coalitions with other urban legislators. In the absence of strong unified urban political coalitions, it is hard to change policies. If they cannot have a substantial impact on major policies, urban legislators have little by way of a track record at home. With an insufficient grasp of policy issues and an inability to influence major policies, why talk to voters about these matters? Better to focus on symbolic issues with visceral appeal, like locking up criminals, or non-policy issues like broken streetlamps.

There is also the matter of race. Luria and Rogers describe white racism as a primary cause for anti-urban bias historically and suggest that it can be overcome by understanding common economic interests. This optimistic view ignores the structural aspects of racial hegemony embedded in our political system, and consequently overlooks the role that African-Americans must themselves play in the fate of cities. Why should whites change their racial practices, and who is going to make them? The notion that white Americans will rebel against anti-urban policies because they are immoral and anti-majority rings hollow, particularly given African-American history. The dispositive political question is not whether policies are bad for the majority, but whether they are bad for the majority of whites. Can a majority of whites be moved to think of their destiny as tied to that of African-Americans and other minorities? This is the critical issue in the metropolitan political mix. It may be no accident that movements toward regionalized urban government and policymaking have had their greatest success in the Midwest, where white populations are most dominant within regions. The argument that economic self-interest will prevail over racism when moral arguments fail is an old one. But history teaches us that white America will not change its habits simply on its own. Democratic advances have always—and especially in this century—required strong African-American participation and leadership.

The need for African-American leadership and mass participation in the quest for democratic advances sharply raises the issue of black leadership and power in cities. As to both, the current situation is dismal. I do not mean this as a personal criticism of black elected officials; universal failure cannot be personal. The problem is historical and structured into our political system. In our nation's history, African-Americans have had little experience in democracy and hence in deciding policy. What little power and policy-making experience they have gained has been recent and concentrated in cities. The lack of policy experts who can translate African-American aspirations into technical criteria is a profound weakness that has handicapped black administrations and legislators across the country. Even more important, two hundred years of racial exclusion in policy making has so deeply embedded racial discrimination within the fabric of our transportation, housing, education, corporate, electoral, and media structures that such discrimination has come to be accepted as a natural state of affairs. I therefore could not agree more with Luria and Rogers that politicizing public policy is of critical importance.

Why haven't black elected officials, the bulk of whom are legislators, been doing this? Why isn't a movement already evident in the black community? I would suggest that African-American legislators suffer from the "retrograde representation" syndrome that I described earlier. Given the situation at its worst, African-American legislators in majority black districts are reduced to a brittle, barren, and anti-democratic symbolic nationalism, one that substitutes identity for issues and demonizes all political competition. Equally retrograde is the "deracialized" black politics adopted by some black candidates who abandon black voters' core issues to attract white voters. No wonder so many inner-city African-Americans are cynical and don't vote.

Is there a treatment for the retrograde representation syndrome, and a role for black politics in the metropolitan future? I think so. Reviving local democratic institutions is the bridge to a shared New Agenda. Here is the first step: devolve governmental functions from the city level to the community level. This is a broad demand. Although not absolute, it is crucial. We need a different model for how government should work, one that increases efficacy and at the same time gives citizens more control over local government. The new model would move the authority to allocate resources to the community level—which means that quality administrators would be paid to build strong community institutions that understand the residents and conditions of their neighborhoods. These local institutions would reach out to regional businesses and government service agencies to connect residents with outside resources and opportunities. The government model we use now, with its large centralized bureaucracies that are disconnected from communities, creates chaos and confusion within those communities. For example, duplication of social services in some poor neighborhoods results in some kids getting the same vaccinations four or five times from different agencies, while other kids are completely overlooked. Moreover, big bureaucracies are seldom responsive to local lawmakers, making both the agencies and the elected leaders unaccountable and functionally corrupt, and rendering local democracy largely superfluous.

The current political climate and recent legislative trends—"welfare-to-work" laws, for example—make the devolution of some government functions to the community level feasible. The welfare-to-work legislation requires persons on welfare to find employment. Moving people off welfare (after skimming off the easy cases) will require intensive case management, accessing drug treatment resources, day care, medical assistance, education and training programs, and providing other services connecting the unemployed to employers. All of these services must be integrated to make the system work. Such hands-on management and system integration is beyond the capacity of mega-bureaucracies. Quality institutions are urgently needed at the community level. Moreover, to be effective, such local institutions have to connect themselves to regional businesses (and jobs) from the outset. Elected officials should be made accountable for the performance of these local agencies. If the agencies are situated in the community, local officials will have difficulty avoiding their responsibility.

I suggest these measures as a beginning for a renewed emphasis on local democracy that goes way beyond elections—to the creation of locally grounded, accessible, and accountable public institutions that can make a difference in the day-to-day lives of ordinary people. Such a vision is especially needed for African-Americans, who fought so hard for the right to vote and are now so disappointed with the results. African-American elected officials and other central-city legislators can help lead the way to a metropolitan future. To do so, they need the help of school principals, police captains, welfare administrators, and housing managers who are fully accountable to community residents—through their locally elected officials. When local legislators are made substantively accountable for the quality of local schools, police, housing, and other municipal services, there will indeed be a politicizing of local policies led by those communities now least active in metropolitan politics. Those with the greatest stake in this fundamental transformation must themselves show that it is possible.

The Real Case for Density

MARGARET WEIR

*A*t least since the 1950s, concern about the pattern of sprawl in metropolitan areas has sparked calls for reform. Critics have charged that sprawl is irrational, promotes racial inequality, and wastes public resources. Luria and Rogers give an old argument a new twist by tying the case against suburban sprawl to the quest for the "high road" in production and service delivery. Although their arguments about the benefits of density are not wholly convincing, there are still good reasons to stem sprawl; and despite formidable obstacles, there are some political openings for moving in that direction.

The argument connecting increased density to the high road of economic development is highly contingent. Density and low-road production are perfectly compatible, as are sprawl and high-road production. Many of the most celebrated agglomerations—Massachusetts's Route 128 or California's Silicon Valley, for example—are the classic products of what is conventionally understood as suburban sprawl. Second, many of the measures Luria and Rogers propose for moving to the high road, such as hefty increases in the minimum wage and increased unionization, while laudable, are only loosely related to density. Finally, there is little evidence that by itself density will promote the inclusion of the poor or minorities who are now isolated in cities. In their study of South Brooklyn, Philip Kasinitz and Jan Rosenberg show that local industries refused to hire jobless residents of nearby housing projects, preferring instead to hire immigrant workers who lived on the other side of the borough. Social networks and employer hiring practices, not sheer proximity or distance, are a key factors in the economic and social isolation of the urban poor.[1] Moreover, efforts to increase density and revive cities can backfire: increased land values may simply push the poor out.

What, then, are the benefits of density and are they worth pursuing? Luria and Rogers are on target when they point to the waste of public resources inherent in our current slash-and-burn approach to development. The expense of building new infrastructure in the exurbs and the costs of coping with the deterioration in declining areas are compelling grounds for stemming sprawl. So are the environmental dangers. Unregulated development that situates new housing in floodplains, on earthquake faults, and in the center of other fragile natural habitats is costly, dangerous, and destructive. Finally, density may ease the patterns of metropolitan inequality by limiting the segmentation of public resources and promoting voice rather than exit as a way to address public problems.

How, then, can we promote denser patterns of development? Luria and Rogers believe the case for density is so persuasive on the grounds of material interest that they do not probe the problem of political will sufficiently. But the barriers should not be underestimated. From George Washington's activities as a land surveyor in Virginia to Bill Clinton's hapless investments on the White River in Arkansas, land speculation has been one of the most lucrative and politically protected undertakings of the powerful. Add suburban politicians who play the race card to promote separatism—regardless of the longer-term interests of their constituents—and urban politicians fearful of losing power in regional entities, and the political alliance for preserving the status quo is impressive. Still, I think there are three promising routes to push the metropolitan agenda forward that particularly address the question of suburban resistance.

One is the federal government. The federal budget impasse and the political weakness of cities halted President Clinton's early efforts to increase spending on cities. But support for metropolitan strategies grew within the Clinton administration, culminating in 1999 in proposals to promote "smart growth" and support city/suburban regional economic partnerships. While the fate of these initiatives is uncertain because they require congressional support, other initiatives can be implemented through federal administrative channels. These include efforts to reverse the harm that the federal government has inflicted on cities by major infrastructure decisions such as the siting of federal facilities. Many of these metropolitan initiatives may remain at the talking stage for some time, but they provide an opening wedge for transforming the federal government from an agent of sprawl to a force favoring density.

A second agent that could press for limiting sprawl is the environmental movement. In the 1970s, environmental organizations were ambivalent when Congress repeatedly considered and failed to pass a National Land Use Act that would have encouraged the states to shape development. At that time, environmentalists had a different agenda, pursuing federal regulation and wilderness protection. Today there is more recognition among environmentalists of the damage to the environment caused by suburban sprawl. There is also a keener sense of the limits of federal regulation and a new interest in "sustainable development." Both are promising trends, not least because of the sympathy that environmental goals arouse among people who live in suburbs. But to make these new orientations among environmentalists more politically salient at the metro level, the environmental movement needs to strengthen its local chapters. For too long, environmentalists have focused their attention on Washington without nurturing the local bases that are needed to pursue environmental goals today.

Finally, there is a broad self-interest argument for increasing density. A significant portion of Americans are frustrated with the lives they lead in our decentralized metropolitan areas. A common argument made by proponents of the current pattern of development is that this is what people want. In fact, there is considerable frustration with the consequences of the current form of suburban development, including hours spent in traffic and the social isolation that contemporary suburban life fosters. These complaints have given rise to the "new urbanism," evident so far primarily in upscale developments such as Disney's Celebration. Yet there is no reason that these same ideas—promoting denser development, community interaction, and housing offered for a range of income levels—cannot be used to promote urban and inner-ring suburban redevelopment, perhaps at a somewhat lower density than in the past. Offering more choice at the center reduces the attraction of the exit options, breaking the spiral of urban and suburban decline that has harmed American metropolitan areas.

Hopeful as this political horizon is, our optimism must be balanced with a cautionary note. One of the central promises of density is that it will improve the lives of the urban poor. Yet the easiest path to "smart growth" and urban revitalization may not only leave the poor out, it may actually harm them. Among the possible consequences of urban revitalization are rising rents, crime control strategies that emphasize prison over opportunity, and the diversion of public funds to high-end amenities designed to appeal to the middle class. These dangers underscore the need for an inclusive and open political process to chart the path toward future metropolitan development. If metropolitan strategies are to help diminish the sharp racial and economic divisions that now mark American metro areas, they must identify and build upon common interests in a racially inclusive decision-making process.

The Need for Coalition

MYRON ORFIELD

*I*n their very impressive article "Metro Futures," Daniel Luria and Joel Rogers seek to connect the nascent regional movement with a more effective economic development strategy that seeks to improve the economy and promote individual opportunity. I know more about regionalism than economic development, so I will concentrate my remarks on the former.

Luria and Rogers argue that cities are important and that it is important to stop their decline for reasons of morality and economic cost. Both are valid concerns. However, the most compelling political motivation for such an effort comes from the rapid decline of inner-ring suburbs, the stagnant nature of blue-collar developing suburbs, and the consequent politics of self-interest.

Contrary to popular belief, socioeconomic instability does not stop neatly at central-city borders. As it crosses into inner suburbs, especially into suburbs that were once blue-collar and middle-class neighborhoods, it accelerates and intensifies. Older working-class suburban communities have less hopeful prospects than the cities they surround. Though central cities get hit first by so-

cial and economic change, they have a fiscal, governmental, and social infrastructure to slow these powerful
trends. In contrast, the inner suburbs lack the central
city's business district, elite neighborhood tax base, social welfare and police infrastructure, and network of
organized political activity. Once the trouble hits, they
often decline far more rapidly.

Further, while "favored-quarter" suburbs (generally
25–35 percent of the population of a metropolitan region)
get virtually all of the new development infrastructure
and truly prosper, the patterns of metropolitan polar-
ization play a cruel joke on most middle- and lower-
middle-income families seeking a better life at the edge
of the region. As they flee the socioeconomic disloca-
tions of the central cities and inner suburbs, they arrive
in rapidly growing school districts with small tax bases.
Because the tax base is inadequate in many such communities and their neighborhoods have throngs of young
children needing to go to school, their local governments
will build almost anything that stands, simply to pay the
bills. Perhaps in part because of overcrowding and mini-
mal spending per pupil, these districts have some of the
highest dropout and lowest college attendance rates in
their regions.

Despite all these troubles, however, the creation of
a coalition between the central cities and inner, low-
tax-base suburbs is no mean feat. These middle-income
(often working-class) suburbs, which have collectively

been a loose cannon politically since 1968, hold the balance of power on regional issues and, arguably, on most political issues in the United States. Our most distinguished political commentators have written about the central significance of this group in holding and maintaining a ruling political coalition.

On the merits, these middle-income, blue-collar suburbs are the largest prospective winners in regional reform. To them, tax-base sharing means lower property taxes and better services, particularly better-funded schools. Regional housing policy means, over time, fewer units of affordable housing crowding their doorsteps. Once understood, this combination is unbeatable. Standing in the way of this coalition, however, are powerful long-term resentments and distrust, based on class and race and fueled by every political campaign since Hubert Humphrey lost the White House in 1968 and Archie Bunker became a Republican.

I think this is the central problem: rebuilding a spatial and economic coalition between the central city and the struggling suburbs and their residents. I think that such a coalition would promote both regionalism and economic reform. But, for the reasons I have mentioned, we have our work cut out for us.

As to the second broad thrust of Luria and Rogers's article—high-road versus low-road development—I need to be educated. As a practical politician, I have been disgusted with low-road strategies. But I have also been hard put to tell poor, struggling communities, from which all economic activity is leaving, to wait for a better policy or not to act. Here we need a concrete transitional program. Further, I believe but do not know that solving these problems will require a powerfully reinvigorated labor movement; that as the world economy becomes more and more integrated, we must use some of the profits generated by our position within it to educate and train our workforce and cushion the impact of the transition; and that a metropolitan and national policy that discourages bidding wars between cities, states, and suburbs and leads to equity among jurisdictions could help. We need more discussion on these issues. Luria and Rogers are to be commended for starting it.

Labor's Role

RICHARD A. FELDMAN

*I*n their analysis of the roots of urban decline, Daniel Luria and Joel Rogers focus attention on American public policy. Their claims about the importance of policy in explaining decline are debatable: one could argue that out-migration from cities has been a norm in the United States for a hundred years; that the federal government supported decentralization to increase survivability in the event of a nuclear attack; or that real estate developers, mortgage interest deductions, and Internal Revenue Code homeseller capital-gains treatment combined have had a far bigger effect than regional economic development policy.[1] But whatever its causes, the current pattern of urban decline (including deunionization and deindustrialization) is disastrous for workers: loss of livable-wage jobs, longer commutes to lower-paying jobs, higher housing costs, and sprawl-induced environmental degradation of water, land, and air. We have no choice but to do what we can within our regions to change this pattern.

Luria and Rogers are right to think there are real possibilities for building coalitions in support of such regional efforts. In Seattle, for example, labor (through the King County Labor Council, AFL-CIO, and the Seattle–King County Building Trades Council, AFL-CIO) has actively supported growth management laws. That support put us on the same side of the table as rural anti-sprawl activists and environmentalists working to preserve open space and farms by fighting green-field development, as well as good-government advocates; we were opposed by the usual array of subdivision developers, mall-meisters, and corporate land-use lawyers. Labor's position was that growth management protected and supported our scarce industrial land and its unionized livable-wage job base. We were also successful in catalyzing the multiparty Duwamish Coalition to address water quality, land contamination, and job retention issues in Seattle's industrial heartland.

So alliances on economic strategy are possible, and they are important. But building them will require work: they will not happen if we think that lots of people are aimlessly milling around, mutually antagonizing each other, waiting for an enterprising leader to pick up the flag and snap them into concerted action in pursuit of their own interests. Labor in particular has much work to do building bridges and bases before we can depend on self-interest to bind us into a grand alliance. The problem is that labor is not now thought of as a natural part of an anti-sprawl alliance, nor in some cases is it ready to take part in that alliance. The sources of the trouble—some of which are now being addressed—lie within both organized labor and the larger community.

The central problem within the labor movement is that labor's traditional contact with cities—through Central Labor Councils (CLCs) coordinating the efforts of different regional unions—was left to wither and die as Washington, D.C.–centered activity came to dominate the political scene in general and labor in particular. This is now changing. With the leadership of Sweeney, Trumka, and Chavez-Thompson, the AFL-CIO is committed to rebuilding the labor movement's connection to its grass roots by encouraging the reemergence of CLCs and by making sure that these CLCs reflect the diversity of their communities. The strength of this commitment is expressed in the Union Cities Resolution recently adopted by the AFL-CIO's Executive Council. This resolution represents a fundamental change in the roles and responsibilities of CLCs to support organizing, political action, coalition building, and other strategic goals of the labor movement. Most importantly for my comments here, the Union Cities Resolution explicitly recognizes the importance of community economic development strategies and of the role of CLCs in building community alliances to promote such strategies and fight corporate subsidy abuse.[2]

In developing those alliances, labor will need to open itself fully to central-city black, Latino, and Asian populations, get back on the radar screen of urban activists, and bridge the divide that currently separates worker rights and human rights groups. Because of the declining numbers of unionized workers, a whole generation of activists have no direct experience with unions through their families or communities. Illegal firing of workers for concerted activity is not on the top of their list of issues. Labor itself bears principal responsibility for changing this situation: (re)introducing people to labor basics is essential. Again there is hope on this front with the preliminary actions taken by the new AFL-CIO leadership: Union Summer, "America Needs a Raise" town hall meetings, and labor teach-ins are all outward-focused, community-oriented actions. We will need to do much more.

What strategies of community economic development will these alliances adopt? Not what Luria and Rogers call CEDS (conventional economic development strategy), for all the reasons that they give. What is unique about their proposal is the role of labor in it. Progressives working to counter urban unemployment and alienation from labor markets are boundlessly creative in developing business-oriented programs—to provide employers with screened and trained employees, to establish suburban job links, or to encourage small business capital formation. In contrast, discussions of labor are all too often confined to strategies for getting building trades jobs for community residents on major development projects.[3] Unions are something to be acted on;

they are not seen as Luria and Rogers see them, as partners in efforts to increase economic opportunity. (We will know that we have arrived when the Aspen Institute or the Casey Foundation publishes a study on innovative ways to increase unionization in low-wage industries, the use of Taft-Hartley trusts to fund housing for hotel workers, or the use of economically targeted investments by pension funds.) Labor needs to creatively and boldly define how it will organize in the community to promote social and economic justice for all working people. But it will not be able to do this properly if it operates in a vacuum or is neglected by other potential allies.

Labor's own revitalization needs to be directly linked to urban revitalization. Luria and Rogers have taken an important step by presenting a program of metro reconstruction that includes such linkage. But let's not assume that economic self-interest alone lines people up behind such a program. We have some important political work to do in developing and understanding each other's interests and potentials before the grand (and necessary) alliance will be fully realized.

Cities in the New Economy

GLENN YAGO

*P*olitical centralization and financial and industrial concentration were the core processes of twentieth-century urban planning, design, and administration; they were also their undoing. Centralized planning policies, drained of democratic participation, promoted this process. Both political and corporate bureaucracies, separately and together, lost the flexibility of more adaptable, competitive, and democratic forms of organization, a flexibility necessary to cope with drastically changed urban economic conditions. In "Metro Futures," Daniel Luria and Joel Rogers make an important contribution to our thinking on this issue.

The stark contrast between abandoned neighborhoods and isolated suburbs redefined cities spatially and emptied urban civic culture. Ironically, the economic, technological, and political conditions sustaining these unworkable arrangements are changing, and the possibilities of urban revitalization can now be restored. The arguments of Luria and Rogers contribute to a debate on how this could occur. Policies which subsidized political, spatial, and social fragmentation in housing, transportation, and urban development have increasingly proven to defy both fiscal responsibility and economic rationality (not to mention common sense). The limits of past urban policies are being increasingly realized on a nonpartisan basis.

The rapid growth of globalization and international trade, the economic energy of growing immigrant and minority communities, the emerging new demographic urban majority, and the rise of "information age" industries create new opportunities for cities. Cities can restructure to service regional and global markets. They can do so now by relying less on vast corporate bureaucracies than ever before in this century, given the shifts in information technology and industrial organization favoring flexible, innovative, and entrepreneurial firms that invest in the skills, talents, and tools that can increase productivity.

As in the past, cities are uniquely suited to retain the distinctive functions of the preindustrial era as centers of culture, artisanship, and commerce. Changes in technological and industrial clusters, which increasingly favor smaller-sized, more flexible and competitive enterprises, suggest renewed growth opportunities for cities. Corporate bureaucracies and heavy manufacturing were clearly the job losers over the past decades in U.S. cities. Reviving cities can now associate themselves with the fastest-growing segments of the new economy— entertainment, multimedia, theming, and small-scale specialized manufacturing and distribution and trade sectors.[1]

How to democratize these urban recoveries is the theme of Luria and Rogers's essay and a topic deserving of further development and policy debate. The persistence of monolithically governed urban political structures makes urban policy hostile to the realities of today's new economy. By continually subsidizing large corporations, particularly when they threaten to leave a given area, at the expense of entrepreneurial firms increasingly run by immigrants, minorities, and women, urban policies provide an incentive for clinging to the past at the expense of the future. The future lies not in subsidizing firms, directly or indirectly, that are not creating new jobs, but in cultivating companies and industries for which the location, workforce characteristics, and cultural institutions of the cities are not a detriment but a positive attraction.

A case in point is provided by the lessons learned before and after the L.A. riots of 1992. Initially, the approach to the South Central area was "top-down"—that is, focused on securing substantial outside private- and public-sector investments, in large part by major corporations. Like most top-down strategies that characterized urban policy in the past, this approach proved unworkable and too fragmented. By 1994, a new strategy emerged, focusing on economic development and spinning off programs that addressed other important social ills. This "bottom-up" strategy sought to determine what the residents in the neglected communities needed. Local industry surveys and community needs assessments were conducted as the basis for a revitalization strategy.

The resulting strategy focused on the formation of manufacturing networks and on retail revitalization of vacant lots. This encouraged small and medium-sized manufacturing companies already located in the target neighborhoods to join together in cooperative endeavors and thereby increase the number of jobs within neglected communities. Also, post-riot vacant lots were transformed into new commercial facilities. Textile and apparel production, ethnic-food processing, furniture manufacturing, and biomedical services all grew substantially, which created jobs and increased home and business ownership in the South Central area. The revitalization of vacant lots has begun to close the retail gap in these neighborhoods as well. But nationwide, cities and neighborhoods like South Central Los Angeles remain largely untapped and ignored both as production bases and as potential markets, despite the structural conditions of the economy that could enable their recovery.[2]

An important theme that must be considered in the emerging urban policy debate is the democratization of capital. Minority-owned businesses have grown explosively over the past ten years (at double the rate of all firms in the U.S. economy), both in numbers of new firms and total sales; they now represent two million firms with total sales of $265 billion.[3] The synergies created by the changing demographics of cities and a rapidly growing minority business infrastructure present a myriad of investment opportunities for the financial community—a potential for growth and development that could be supported by effective urban policies. Despite its promise, this emerging market continues to be overlooked and untapped due to misperceptions and lack of information. Demand for capital remains unsatisfied. The information and financial technologies and innovations are at hand to develop this sector of our economy. Within the policy frame ably developed by Luria and Rogers, it is long past time that we seized the opportunity to do so.

❧ I I I ❧

Reply

DANIEL D. LURIA AND JOEL ROGERS

$\mathcal{T}$hese generous and thoughtful comments show broad agreement with the economic and policy arguments we make in "Metro Futures": that metropolitan regions warrant attention as economic units and metro reconstruction will benefit the nation as a whole as well as the occupants of cities; that federal and state policies should be changed to remove subsidies to sprawl and interregional competition for business; that local governments should break with conventional development strategies and focus on building the infrastructure of high-road economic performance. And they concur with our argument that high-road administration requires a much more active role in the economy for popular organizations (beginning with organizations of workers), and with our central claim that inner-ring suburbanites and central-city residents have common material interests sufficient to underwrite a political alliance. From as diverse a group as this, that is a striking level of agreement.

If the commentators have a collective reservation, it is about our apparent slighting of the barriers to building the high-road metro coalition and securing meaningful contributions from its presumptive component parts. Phil Thompson notes many hard reasons—from the irrationalities of present political structures to the embedded economics of racism—why suburban and central city politicians have not gotten together on this project. Myron Orfield, reporting from the trenches, cautions us about the volatility of inner-ring suburban partners in a metro reconstruction effort—even as he affirms their economic stake in its success even more forcefully than we. Rich Feldman reminds us that labor will need some time to dig itself out of its present hole, and that doing so requires change not just in the scope and scale of union activity, but in its structure and politics. Bruce Katz cautions us about the dysfunction and "downtown boosterism" of many central city governments and their bureaucracies. Glenn Yago offers a case study of the natural reactionary impulses of local elites, even "do-gooder" ones. And Margaret Weir has seen too many destructive initiatives nominally undertaken on behalf of the central city poor to believe that our prescriptions will automatically help them.

Well and good. We agree the fight will be hard, the politics inevitably messy, and that the truth is in the details—with the all-important "detail" of actually showing benefit to the truly needy requiring eternal vigilance in its pursuit. A new metro politics will inevitably stumble over material conflicts on the way to getting to common material gain. The internal politics of coalition partners—which do indeed need to change—will inevitably slow progress toward their joining together cooperatively. And besides making cities habitable and attractive to the middle class, we need also to widen opportunities for those not yet in that class.

Accepting all this, we would offer two points in reply.

First, what is less apparent in these commentaries is an appreciation of the potential of high-road strategies themselves to reduce some of the obstacles they face. To take only the most obvious example, consider business opposition. Today, those interested in improving life in our cities generally face a business community that seems unified, at least in public. This unity is a sham. Chambers of commerce and similar bodies represent the lowest-common denominator of their constituents —which effectively means the interests of the lowest-roaders among them—as "the business position." But in fact, as we argue in our piece, a significant fraction of business does not share in those interests. The strategy we recommend amounts to an invitation to this latter group to admit that fact, break (at least on this) with their brethren, and avail themselves of the substantial popular political support that high-road policies would enjoy. If this course were to be taken by even a limited number of firms, we imagine the political dynamics of progressive metro reconstruction would change considerably. Instead of being seen as inevitably antibusiness, the project of reconstruction would be seen as offering choices, with contention within the business sector itself about how business ought to be done.

Second and separately, whatever the political difficulties our proposed project would face, the real political question is whether these difficulties are so severe that we should reject the project we have outlined for another. And here the answer—unamended by the commentators—seems clearly to be no. So we are left with broad agreement: metro reconstruction is urgently needed; the means and material base for making it happen are at hand; the effort will require organization and the breaking of some rotten political eggs, but the broad direction and essentials of the project can be envisioned and have been reasonably stated here; and there is no more attractive alternative. For us, that is more than enough agreement to warrant getting started in earnest.

Metro reconstruction is not just a nice idea. It is central to a productive, egalitarian, and democratic future for our nation. Those moved by these values should recognize this fact and focus more clearly on realizing the possibilities this project describes. And with urban squalor and inequality little changed by the nation's otherwise exuberant economy, we need to do it now.

Notes

DANIEL D. LURIA AND JOEL ROGERS / *Metro Futures*

1. About 80 percent of Americans live in what the Census Bureau terms "Metropolitan Statistical Areas" (MSAs). MSAs include not only central cities and their working-class suburbs, but outer-ring "bedroom suburbs" as well. There is no standard, accepted definition of the "inner ring"—communities contiguous with the central city that are mostly working-class, mixed-use entities with historic ties to the central core—but our research on Milwaukee and Detroit suggests that nationwide, as of the late 1980s, at least 65 percent of the MSA population lives in inner-ring suburbs or in the central cities themselves.

2. This essay draws on our past collaboration with other members of the Midwest Consortium for Economic Development Alternatives (MCEDA). See *Metro Futures: A High-Wage, Low-Waste, Democratic Development Strategy for America's Cities and Inner Suburbs* (New York and Madison, Wisc.: Sustainable America and Center on Wisconsin Strategy, 1996). More recently, we have benefited from countless conversations with others active in promoting high-road metropolitan solutions to our urban ills, including many of those commenting on this essay here. This essay appeared in slightly different form in *Boston Review* 22 (February–March 1997), as part of its New Democracy Forum series.

3. More recently, welfare reform and the implementation of the federal balanced budget bill will impose further costs on working-class suburbs, and will cost cities even more.

4. This calculation comes from a study of fifty-nine metropolitan areas. See H. V. Savitch, David Collins, Daniel Sanders, and John P. Markham, "Ties That Bind: Central Cities, Suburbs, and the New Metropolitan Region," *Economic Development Quarterly* 7 (Novem-

ber 1993): 341–57. The study notes that the share of suburban income associated with central city density and income increased substantially over the 1979–87 period observed, suggesting tighter linkage. See as well Richard Voith, "City and Suburban Growth: Substitutes or Complements?" *Business Review* (Federal Reserve Bank of Philadelphia), September–October 1992: 31. Voith finds that in the Northeast and Midwest, over the past two decades the relationship between city and suburban population growth has turned from negative to positive: slower population loss (or even gain) in cities is associated with higher suburban growth.

5. While internationalization is very important, we believe it has been exaggerated as a bar to the sort of reconstructive program offered here. Most U.S. manufacturers buy and sell overwhelmingly to themselves, and the long-term trend of the U.S. economy is toward service providers, usually not traded on even a national basis, much less internationally. Even when competition is international, alternative strategies with very different social consequences are available. Choices between them can be shaped by factors clearly under popular control. Even the diminished states, as we shall see, hold many cards.

6. Thus far, it appears, this effect survives the advent of the Internet and other advanced communications technology. Despite the fact that phone lines and modems put rural areas in the digital loop (witness the profusion of bills-processing centers in rural places), the higher the knowledge content of the information involved, the larger the premium on colocation. In Michigan, for example, fear of the UAW and the "bad business climate" that its continuing (if muted) political clout has been able to preserve have driven the state's share of major auto-supplier manufacturing facilities to less than 10 percent of the North American total. Yet twenty-six of the top thirty independent supplier companies (all with sales exceeding $1 billion annually) have technical centers within twenty miles of downtown Detroit. Every day, thousands of employees of these centers interact with engineers at GM, Ford, and Chrysler, and with many of the smaller high-road shops that will make the equipment and tooling that workers around the world will use to make their products.

7. *Business Week*, 2 November 1998, 22. The article reviewed a re-

cent study by Regional Financial Associates that found (among other things) that businesses that relocated operations from rural to urban areas experienced sharp increases in productivity.

8. Among Midwestern males, for example, the share of whites employed in durable manufacturing declined by a third over the years 1973–1988, from 33 percent to 21 percent; among African-Americans, it declined by three-quarters over the same time period, from 42 to 13 percent. With manufacturing jobs generally paying better than service-sector ones, this trend had huge effects on black earnings.

9. *TechnEcon: Research Newsletter of Automation and American Manufacturing* (Fall 1989), published by the Industrial Technology Institute, Ann Arbor, Michigan.

10. The PBS data show several characteristics of high-road shops that mark a statistically significant difference from their low-road competitors: more capital investment, less dependence on intermediate goods production, more design contribution, more focus on producing assemblies rather than loose parts, greater integration of production and quality assurance, more routine quoting of jobs that include responsibility to design and build tooling, broader computer use and programming by shop workers, higher levels of worker training, more real teamwork and information sharing, and enforceable worker rights.

MARGARET WEIR / *The Real Case for Density*

1. Philip Kasinitz and Jan Rosenberg, "Missing the Connection: Social Isolation and Employment on the Brooklyn Waterfront," *Social Problems* 43, no. 2 (May 1996): 501–19.

RICHARD A. FELDMAN / *Labor's Role*

1. Section 1034 of the Internal Revenue Code enables homesellers to shelter capital gains only if they purchase a home at least equal in price to the one they have sold. In urban areas, home values (in general) increase with distance from the center; so the provision encour-

ages movement out and away from the cities. A study of the Cleveland area found that 81 percent of homesellers complied with the provision, and of those that complied, 84 percent moved farther out. (Source: "The IRS Homeseller Capital Gain Provision: Contributor to Urban Decline," Ohio Housing Research Network.)

2. The Union Cities Resolution challenges CLCs and their local unions to commit to pursue eight goals:

1. Signing half of its local union affiliates on to a program coordinated with their internationals to shift 30 percent of the local's resources into organizing
2. Developing a rapid-response/solidarity team to support worker struggles in the community
3. Reaching a member growth rate of 3 percent per year by 2000
4. Organizing grassroots labor/community political action committees in each legislative district
5. Sponsoring an economics education program for a majority of affiliated local unions
6. Building public support for the right of workers to join unions by sponsoring a city council resolution and by insisting that candidates pledge to support organizing
7. Ensuring diversity in the entire structure of the CLC
8. Working with community allies on economic development strategies that establish community standards for local industries and public investment

3. See, for example, Cheryl Bardoe, *Employment Strategies for Urban Communities: How to Connect Low-Income Neighborhoods with Good Jobs* (1996).

Glenn Yago / *Cities in the New Economy*

1. Joel Kotkin, *Can the Cities Be Saved?* Milken Institute, 1997.
2. Rebuilding *LA's Urban Communities: A Final Report from RLA*, Milken Institute, 1997.
3. Glenn Yago and Michael Harrington, *Mainstreaming Minority Business: Financing Emerging Domestic Markets*, U.S. Department of Commerce, 1999.

ABOUT THE CONTRIBUTORS

RICHARD A. FELDMAN is executive director of the Seattle Worker Center, economic development and workforce development division of the King County Labor Council, AFL-CIO.

BRUCE KATZ is director of the Brookings Institution's new Center on Urban and Metropolitan Policy, and a senior fellow in its Economic Studies Program. He is the former chief of staff of the U.S. Department of Housing and Urban Development, and the author of *Beyond City Limits: The Case for Metropolitan Solutions to Urban Problems.*

DANIEL D. LURIA is vice president of the Michigan Manufacturing Technology Center, where he directs the Performance Benchmarking Service, the nation's most comprehensive source of information on the performance of small and medium-sized manufacturing firms.

MYRON ORFIELD is a member of the Minnesota House of Representatives and adjunct law professor at the University of Minnesota. He is the director of the Metropolitan Area Program of the American Land Institute and the author of *Metropolitics: A Regional Agenda for Community and Stability.*

JOEL ROGERS is a professor of law, political science, and sociology at the University of Wisconsin/Madison, where he also directs a policy and project development center for "high-road" economic development, the Center on Wisconsin Strategy (COWS). Rogers has written widely on American politics and public policy; his most recent book (with Richard Freeman) is *What Workers Want.*

J. PHILLIP THOMPSON teaches political science at Columbia University. He was formerly director of housing coordination under New York's Mayor David Dinkins, and was a deputy general manager of the New York City Housing Authority.

MARGARET WEIR is professor of sociology and political science at the University of California, Berkeley, and a nonresident senior fellow at the Brookings Institution. She is currently writing a book on the political isolation of cities in the United States.

About the Contributors

GLENN YAGO is director of the Capital Studies Program at the Milken Institute in Santa Monica, California. A former professor of economics at Baruch College and the CUNY Graduate Center, he is an internationally recognized specialist in capital markets, financial institutions, and financial innovation. Yago has written widely on these topics, and on economic development generally, with a focus on transportation policy. He is most recently coauthor (with Michael Harrington) of *Mainstreaming Minority Business: Financing Emerging Domestic Markets.*